BUCKINGHAM PALACE

For the first time in its history,

Buckingham Palace has opened its doors

to the world. This guide

provides an insight into the glittering

rooms, the priceless treasures and

the masterpieces which adorn the home of

the British monarch..

Buckingham Palace is published by Headway, Home and Law Publishing Group Ltd., in London.

© Headway, Home & Law Publishing Group Ltd. 1993. Colour origination: Coloursystems Ltd. Printed by: Severn Valley Press/Chase Webb.

Text: Gardenhouse Editions. Editor: Sue Rose. Design: Mary Ryan.

The exterior of Buckingham Palace on a summer's day

CONTENTS

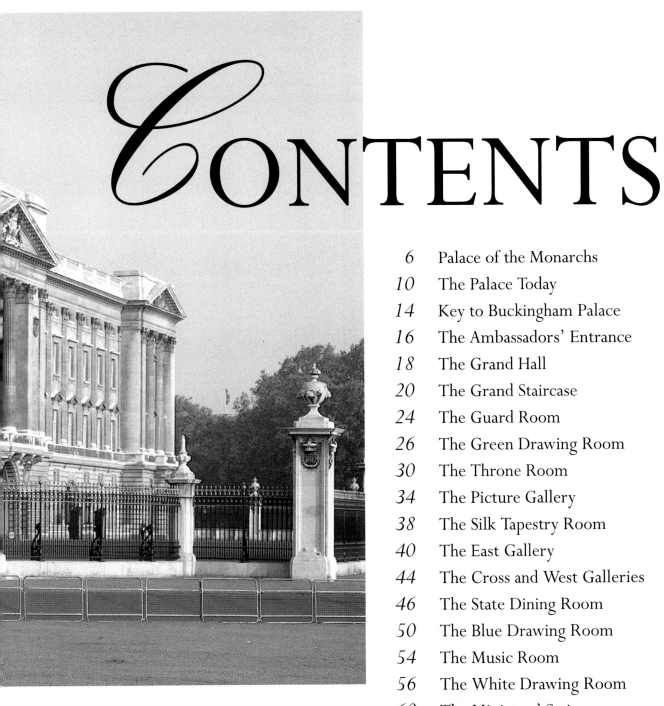

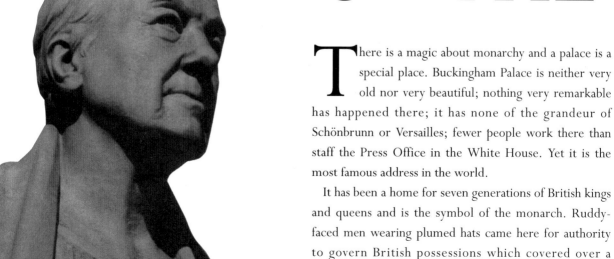

PALACE OF THE M

There is a magic about monarchy and a palace is a special place. Buckingham Palace is neither very old nor very beautiful; nothing very remarkable has happened there; it has none of the grandeur of Schönbrunn or Versailles; fewer people work there than staff the Press Office in the White House. Yet it is the most famous address in the world.

It has been a home for seven generations of British kings and queens and is the symbol of the monarch. Ruddy-faced men wearing plumed hats came here for authority to govern British possessions which covered over a

ONARCHS

quarter of the land surface of the globe. Heads of State, leaders of the Commonwealth, and diplomats are received here today. In times of crisis or celebration, when war, or the death of a monarch seemed inevitable, great silent crowds gazed up at the royal balcony for reassurance that the country was as it had always been. They returned to cheer the fairytale processions in golden coaches for which they still have an affection.

King George IV (1820-30) made it a palace. His father had spent £21,000 on an attractive red brick house, built in 1702 for the Duke of Buckingham and set in meadows,

Queen Victoria   *Edward VII*   *George V*

where he and his wife Queen Charlotte could live apart from the Court in St James's. What had been Buckingham House became known as the Queen's House.

Their son wanted something grander and more up-to-date. After viewing, and rejecting, many magnificent designs from architects of the day for a new palace, George IV asked John Nash to rebuild the house. When it was done he said: "Nash, the State Rooms you have made are so handsome that I think I shall hold my courts there". The architect protested that there were not enough rooms. The King replied: "You know nothing about the matter. It will make an excellent palace."

Nash and his King were both highly intelligent, imaginative men, and many of the treasures to be seen there now were acquired by George IV, but they lacked an interest in project management. The rebuilding cost a fortune and soon after the King's death, Nash was sacked. William IV (1830-37), who succeeded him, hated the place and tried to get the Government to take it as a replacement for the Houses of Parliament which had been burned down in 1834, or even as a barracks. They refused and the Palace remained a Royal home.

Buckingham Palace came into its own as a Royal residence on the accession of Queen Victoria (1837-1901). The eighteen-year-old Queen arrived from Kensington Palace in the state coach, leaving her bossy mother behind. She ignored the bad drains and the incomplete furnishings ('there was furniture enough for her and she did not care for carpets').

Edward VIII

George VI

Elizabeth II

In 1840 she married Prince Albert of Saxe-Coburg-Gotha and Nash's prediction that there were not enough rooms came true. The Palace was soon enlarged to accommodate their growing family and to provide rooms for new functions such as the State Visits by other monarchs which were a 19th-century innovation. In 1847 the architect Edward Blore added the East Front, now instantly recognisable the world over. Balls, concerts and gaiety of all kinds made her early reign delightful.

Victoria's misery at the death of Albert in 1861 plunged Buckingham Palace into 40 years of shrouded decline. The widow lived at Windsor Castle. "Day turned into night," she said. On the few occasions that she had to come to London, Albert's evening clothes were put out as usual.

Her son, King Edward VII (1901-10) introduced electric lighting and other improvements. In 1913, King George V (1910-36) had the familiar East Front faced with Portland stone and added new gates. King Edward VIII (January to December 1936), later the Duke of Windsor, disliked 'the Mausoleum' and simply had an office there.

Throughout the Second World War, his younger brother Albert, called King George VI (1936-52), lived here with Queen Elizabeth (now the Queen Mother) and their two daughters. The Palace was hit nine times by bombs. They lived on wartime rations, shivered with cold and carried gas masks – much like other blitzed Londoners, except they carried loaded pistols and had exiled European kings and queens to stay.

THE $\mathcal{P}$ALACE TODAY

When Her Majesty the Queen is in residence, the Flagman rises at dawn and hoists the Royal Standard over the Palace. On a normal day, a flag 3.6 x 1.8 metres (12 x 6 feet) is flown; there are smaller ones for windy weather and larger ones for special occasions. The moment Her Majesty leaves the Palace, down it comes. At 9am, the Queen's Piper inflates his bagpipes and begins to play beneath her windows for 15 minutes. By

that hour too, all 355 people who work for the Queen in Buckingham Palace will have begun their working day.

In the basement workshops, gilders, cabinet makers and French polishers are at work restoring and repairing; the flower arranger and the carpet planner go about their business; the fender smith sets off to polish the innumerable fireplaces, the clockmakers to wind and adjust the clocks. There are 19 State Rooms in the Palace, 53 Royal and guest

Behind the serene exterior
of the Palace work cooks
and butlers, soldiers and
policemen, carpenters and
plumbers, gardeners and
chauffeurs and two
members of staff whose
role is to wind the 300
clocks each day

bedrooms, 188 staff bedrooms, 92 offices, 78 bathrooms
and lavatories, and 600 rooms in all. Keeping them spot-
less is the job of the 26 housemaids and the 'daily ladies'.
Inside the Palace are a Post Office, handling over 100,000
items a year, a police station and kitchens serving up to
600 meals a day.

On the stroke of 11.30am each day, the guard changes.
The New Guard, three officers and 40 men (fewer if the
Queen is away), which has formed up in Wellington
Barracks, marches across to face the Old Guard in the
forecourt. The officers commanding the Guards march
up and down with the Foot Guards' unique nonchalant
gliding pace, murmuring to one another, while the stamp-
ing business of changing the sentries is done. They touch
hands in a symbolic handing over of keys, and then the
New Guard marches off up the Mall to St James's Palace
(where the guardroom is) behind their corps of drums.

Then perhaps a new ambassador calls, arriving by carriage
to present his credentials 'to the Court of St James's', for
the Court is, strictly speaking, still in the old palace.

The raising of the Royal
Standard signifies that the
Queen is in residence,
above

Left, the Guard outside
the Palace changes each
morning with great
ceremony

From above right, clockwise: acres of glass windows need to be cleaned; a sentry stands guard; the Queen entertains Heads of State from around the world; the Guard marches off up the Mall; and Prince Charles holds one of the 14 annual investitures

Fourteen times a year, the Queen holds an Investiture in the Ballroom when about 140 people are honoured with knighthoods or decorations for merit or gallantry. They receive their decoration from the Sovereign, watched by two members of their family, while a band plays. Two Gurkha soldiers (from Nepal, but still part of the British army) assist the courtiers.

All day, the Members of the Royal Household, the highest-ranking of the Queen's advisors, supported by the lower-ranking Officials, have been engaged in the complex administration of the Palace itself and the monarchy it serves. They make arrangements for the Queen's numerous visits; for the Garden Parties and for state visits to England by other heads of state (the Queen entertains up to 30,000 guests each year); for the press which reports it all; for the Royal Collection Department, which maintains the lustre of art in the royal surroundings; and for the Privy Purse which pays the bills. Mid-afternoon, they stop work and meet for tea.

Once a week, the Prime Minister calls at 6.30pm for an audience. It is an absolutely private exchange of views. Later, if she has no official engagements, the Queen likes to watch TV. Helped by one of the 15 footmen, a Page of the Backstairs will bring supper on a tray up to her first-floor apartment overlooking Green Park.

As night falls, a policeman (in slippers) takes up his post outside the Queen's bedroom door. The sentries leave their boxes and help the police patrol the precincts. It's business as usual again tomorrow at the Palace.

$\mathcal{K}$EY

THE *A*MBASSADORS' ENTRANCE

The Ambassadors' Entrance, formerly known as the Entrée, was once only used by those who had been granted the privilege of 'an entrée': members of the Cabinet, the Diplomatic Corps, former holders of the chief ministerial offices, the Royal Household, and personal friends of the Sovereign. Today it is the entrance for thousands of visitors to the Palace.

On great state occasions, the Queen's coach drives into the Quadrangle and stops at the Grand Entrance. Before the alterations of 1847 added the East Front, the Palace was built around only three sides of the Quadrangle and the Grand Entrance was visible from the 'town' side of the Palace. Trafalgar Square (also conceived by John Nash, the Palace's first architect) could be seen from the windows of the State Apartments on the first floor. This façade was the front of the house, screened only by the Marble Arch, later removed and erected at the end of Oxford Street.

At the centre of the Quadrangle is the portico which conceals the Grand Entrance. Four pairs of squat Ionic columns made of cast-iron support the stone Corinthian columns of the upper storey. Above them, the pediment sculpted by E H Bailey shows Britannia surrounded by Neptune and muscular Tritons. Silhouetted against the sky, figures of Neptune, Commerce and Navigation (made in artificial Coade 'stone') remind the visitor of the basis of Britain's power and glory in the mid-19th century.

In the offices, corridors and flats around three sides of the Quadrangle the workaday business of the Palace is conducted; on the fourth side are the great State Apartments. On the way to the Grand Hall, one passes paintings of the first two Hanoverian kings of England and of Frederick Prince of Wales, whose mother, Queen Caroline, said: "If I was to see him in hell, I should feel no more for him than any other rogue that ever went there."

THE GRAND HALL

A short flight of steps leads state visitors from the Grand Entrance into the Grand Hall. The walls and ceiling are now painted a soft ivory white, but originally the walls were lined with scagliola, a coloured plaster technique intended to look like stone. When the plaster cracked, King William IV, a practical man, had it painted over.

The elegant chairs and benches were made in 1802 for Brighton Pavilion. Four great lanterns which lit the Hall in Nash's day are no longer there, but a pair of French Empire wall lights on either side of the fireplace were given by Queen Mary in 1929.

The Grand Hall, like the rest of the Palace, reflects the changing tastes of generations of Royal occupants. On the overmantel, above the sumptuously carved marble chimney-piece (made in 1829 by Joseph Theakstone), is a modest bust of the first of them, the man whose taste is stamped on every room of the State Apartments, which were built to his orders and filled with objects he had painstakingly collected – King George IV.

On either side of the Hall, shallow flights of broad marble steps, punctuated by the waist-high pedestals supporting coupled columns composed of single blocks of veined Carrara marble, lead up to the principal passage along this side of the Palace (the Marble Hall) and to a fireplace, beside which chilly courtiers could wait, or seek a vantage point above the crowd.

Nash thus fashioned the room into a shallow amphitheatre as an appropriate setting in which to welcome the men in military, diplomatic, or court uniforms, ladies in corresponding finery, foreigners in national dress, and servants in state livery who would fill it on great occasions. But he reserved the most theatrical effect for the fourth side, for here the Grand Staircase rises towards the State Apartments.

THE *G*RAND STAIRCASE

O n 26 September 1829, a team of 17 horses drew what the *Evening Standard* called 'one of the most stupendous blocks of white marble' from a wharf on the Thames at Pimlico towards the works at Buckingham House. It weighed 24 tons and was intended for the Grand Staircase. On the shafts turned from blocks such as this great one, Nash had cast bronze Corinthian capitals fixed and gilded. His palatial staircase fitted exactly within the dimensions of the original domestic one, although Nash curved out the turns at the landing.

Art historians will notice in the spatial complexity of the staircase some echoes of Borromini's Perspectiva in the Palazzo Spada in Rome and even the Scala Regia in the Vatican. The extension towards the second floor was added in the 1850s, making a rather dauntingly long cascade of steps when seen from the Hall. Other changes included the carved swags under the pictures and the Corinthian pilasters in the angles of the walls, added in 1902. The walls, which were first covered with scagliola, then marbled in panels, were redecorated in a plain off-white and the mellow antique colours of antique Italy were replaced by those of a grand French hotel. Yet in the sky light which filters through Wainwright's lovely etched glass, the colours sparkle.

The glory of the Staircase is the balustrade. Made by Samuel Parker of bronze wrought in a flowing design of acanthus scrolls and rosettes with oak leaves, acorns and laurel leaves, it gives a Regency swagger to the standard classical motifs. It is undeniably grand and leads to the first floor of the Palace where most of the magnificent State Rooms are located. One flight ascends ahead to the East Gallery while the curved flights lead to the marble doorway of the Guard Room.

Painted in 1797, when she was 53, this
portrait of Queen Charlotte by Sir
William Beechey depicts her walking near
Frogmore House with her Maltese dog

This 'Cellini' bronze figure of Perseus
and Medusa at the top of the Grand Staircase
is a 19th-century replica

The Grand Staircase boasts 10 royal portraits and some fine figures flanking the steps. Shortly after her Coronation in 1837, Queen Victoria planned this arrangement of royal portraits and it has not been altered since. They are of her immediate ancestors and relations and she intended them to make manifest her succession.

From the top of the stairs, clockwise, they are:

William IV, Victoria's uncle, known as 'The Sailor King', (by Sir Thomas Lawrence).

Prince George of Cumberland, later King George V of Hanover (also by Sir Thomas Lawrence).

Princess Charlotte of Wales, daughter of George IV (after George Dawe).

Leopold I, King of the Belgians. He was the consort of Princess Charlotte and an uncle of Queen Victoria (after George Dawe).

Queen Charlotte, walking with her dog (Sir William Beechey).

George III Victoria's grandfather (Sir William Beechey).

Victoria, Duchess of Kent, Queen Victoria's mother (Sir George Hayter).

Augustus, Duke of Sussex. The sixth son of George III, evidently took to the Scottishness his brother, George IV, had made fashionable (Sir David Wilkie).

Edward, Duke of Kent Queen Victoria's father and the fourth son of George III (George Dawe).

Queen Adelaide, wife of William IV. (Sir Martin Archer-Shee).

The marble statue in the right-hand niche is J Geef's *Love and Malice,* on the left is R J Wyatt's *The Huntress.* They were birthday presents from Queen Victoria to Prince Albert.

Prince George of Cumberland by Sir Thomas Lawrence was painted at Cumberland Lodge in Windsor Great Park when the young prince was nine years old

THE G UARD ROOM

The small oval Guard Room forms an anteroom to the Green Drawing Room. The visitor enters it through the first of a series of great folding mirror doors, present throughout the State Apartments. Made of Spanish mahogany, they are 3.5 metres (12ft) high and 2 metres (7ft) wide. On both sides they bear silvered glass plates – very large for those days – and copious decoration in ormolu (gilt bronze or brass). The metalwork is by Samuel Parker, who made the balustrade on the Grand Staircase. He also made the ornate gilt metal bands surrounding the doorways. The work, though no doubt cast, is carefully hand-finished, with some parts left matt and others burnished to a shine. Above the door are two rectangular panels in low relief by William Pitts which represent Peace and War. The parquetry floor is of East India satinwood. The chamber is lit by a domed skylight, set with 28 glass plates deeply cut with rayed crowns about a Garter star, a smaller and simpler version of the dome over the Grand Staircase.

On the wall of each alcove is a panel (c1730) of Louis XV Gobelins tapestry from the series called *Les Portières des Dieux*. On the left is Venus symbolising Spring and site, Bacchus symbolising Autumn. The X-framed gilt armchairs with reeded frames and lion's paw feet were made in 1826-28 for Windsor Castle by Morel & Seddon. The shape, an imitation of the Roman curule – a folding chair of chariot shape reserved for the highest magistrates – was extremely fashionable in England at the time.

There are six pieces of sculpture, including a standing figure (or 'marble portrait' as the Victorians used to say) of Prince Albert. The statue of Queen Victoria is by John Gibson, a sculptor who liked to tint his stone. His *Tinted Venus* achieved great fame in its day and this portrait of the Queen was originally partly coloured.

THE $\mathcal{G}$REEN DRAWING ROOM

This spacious saloon, 16 metres (53ft) long and 12.5 metres (41ft) wide, is the first of the State Rooms and was intended by King George IV as a place where his visitors would gather before proceeding to the Throne Room beyond. At that time, if the finely-figured concave mahogany shutters were opened, guests could have seen over the trees of St James's Park to the town beyond. After a ball in the 1840s, just before the Quadrangle was enclosed, thus obscuring the view, Queen Victoria stood here to watch the sun rise over St Paul's Cathedral. The windows open onto the loggia over the Grand Entrance and the mirror doors lead to the Picture Gallery.

Elder courtiers of George IV would have known that they were in what had been Queen Charlotte's Saloon during old King George's reign. Their grandfathers would perhaps have known it as the Duke of Buckingham Saloon for it is essentially the same room, thrice decorated, each time in the very latest fashion. When it was re-decorated and furnished in the 1830s Queen Adelaide, wife of William IV, asked that Irish work people should be employed. Accordingly samples of green 'tabinet' (a watered fabric of silk and wool) were sent and one was chosen for the wall-covering. A great Axminster carpet was made the same year for the sum of £138. It is now only laid for state occasions. The curtains and wall-covering are replacements of similar character to the originals.

Around the floors of the State Apartments are a series of inlaid borders in fine woods. This one is of holly and finely-figured satinwood, set in a walnut background. A richly ornamented ceiling supports five cut-glass chandeliers with icicle crystals and faceted drops. The room is light and calm – an ideal place to prepare to meet your Sovereign.

The pot-pourri vase, with
its exquisite detailing, is
perhaps the finest of George
IV's porcelain
collection. It is shown here
against the wall-covering of
the Green Drawing Room,
similar to the original
ordered by Queen Adelaide
in 1834

THE GREEN DRAWING ROOM

The porcelain in this room is all of soft-paste Sèvres and it forms part of the collection made by King George IV, who bought everything of great quality he could find from among the ruins of the French Revolution. It is now ranked as the finest collection of Sèvres in the world and is principally kept in the Palace and at Windsor Castle. The pot-pourri vase shaped like a medieval ship *(vaisseau à mât)*, is emblematic of the city of Paris, and is perhaps the finest piece amongst this collection. It probably belonged to Madame de Pompadour, Louis XV's greatly loved mistress. It is dated 1758 and was bought just after the Napoleonic Wars.

To one side stands a particularly fine Louis XVI ebony and ormolu cabinet, made in about 1785 by Adam Weisweiler and enriched with panels of *pietra dura* (inlay of hard, often semi-precious, stones). However, these panels were made a century earlier, in Florence and at the Gobelins manufactory in France. Look too for the ebony and gilt bronze chest of drawers by Martin Carlin, for the same is true of this piece also. Two of the panels have scratched on the back the name of G A Giachetti who was employed by Louis XIV to make mosaic panels. The chest previously belonged to the singer Marie-Joséphine Laguerre around 1775.

Two French cabinets on either side as one enters are veneered with tortoise-shell on pewter, and vice versa, known as *contre-partie* marquetry.

The grand piano, 'Patent Sostinente Piano Forte', is the instrument which gave its name to the Music Room, in which it stood for many years. King George IV bought it for Brighton Pavilion in 1820 from Isaac Mott of Pall Mall, London.

Of the seven portraits of Royal offspring and relations the earliest is that of Isabella Clara Eugenie and Catharina, daughters of Philip II of Spain, attributed to Sofonisba Anguissola c1569.

THE *T*HRONE ROOM

T he State Apartments of Buckingham Palace, like those of other palaces built before it, start with a series of chambers of ascending importance through which those seeking formal audience of the Monarch had to pass. They culminate in the appropriately magnificent Throne Room. Here, those whom social position or good fortune allowed would find the Sovereign enthroned; a person of power unimaginable in modern times, dispensing honours, disposing of livings and ruling over the state and its empire. It glitters with the glamour of majesty and does not attempt to conceal the symbols of maritime and terrestrial power.

The Royal Alcove, in which the thrones are set, is flanked with carved and gilded piers, supporting massive trusses from which two winged figures of Victory by Bernasconi spring like the figure-heads of men-of-war. Like those supporting the bust of King William IV (himself a sailor) in the tympanum of the main doorway, they commemorate the battles of Trafalgar and Waterloo. The gilt garlands they hold like reins dip beneath the arch and lead the eye to a rayed medallion.

The friezes around the walls are by E H Bailey (1828). Romantic, rather than historical, they depict scenes from the Wars of the Roses: the Battle of Tewkesbury; the marriage of Henry VII; the Battle of Bosworth; and, on the south side, Bellona, Goddess of War and a group of warriors.

The deeply coved ceiling, supporting a shallow dome, is beautifully ornamented with shields bearing the elements of the Royal Arms in painted and gilt plaster relief. It is one of the finest early 19th-century examples in existence. Until 1902, the splendid scene was lit by 250 wax candles in the seven great chandeliers that are exceptional both in size and quality.

The Horatii Clock
is symbolic of the themes of the Throne Room

THE *Throne* ROOM

*The gilt Council Chair,
inspired by the chariots of Rome*

The initialled throne chairs on the platform are those used by Her Majesty the Queen and HRH The Duke of Edinburgh during the 1953 Coronation. They were made in that year by White, Allom & Co. The smaller thrones on either side were made by the same firm and were used by King George VI (the Queen's father) and Her Majesty Queen Elizabeth the Queen Mother at their Coronation in 1937.

Hanging beside the throne are four gilt wood trophies. They are probably by French craftsmen working in England at the end of the 18th century and come from the Old Throne Room at Carlton House.

Standing on the mantelpiece is one of the most striking timepieces in the Palace. It dates from the early 19th century and wonderful ormolu work depicts the scene in Jacques-Louis David's painting, *The Oath of the Horatii*, 'the archetypal picture of purist neo-classicism'. The picture's moral, appropriate to the room with its emblems of might, is about duty to one's country in battle.

On either side of the clock are candelabra of gilt and patinated bronze in the form of cornucopias (horns of plenty), ending in a stag's and boar's head respectively. The reliefs on their marble bases represent Commerce and Industry. They were bought in 1814.

The Council Chair in the window bay is one of a pair made in 1812 for the Throne Room at Carlton House. Shaped like Roman chariots, they have been described as 'the finest examples of Regency furniture extant'.

The single portrait in the Throne Room is of the Duchess of Brunswick, painted in 1767 by Angelica Kauffman.

*The rayed medallion in regal scarlet and gold
which hangs above the thrones*

THE $\mathcal{P}$ICTURE GALLERY

The Picture Gallery is not as John Nash intended it. His roof was an elaborate construction, reminiscent of medieval timber-work, opened to allow some 24 glazed domes along either wall, while down the centre, a long row of square pitched skylights let in more light. In the 1850s, when Queen Victoria used the gallery for banqueting, the roof was decorated in red, blue and gold – making it more in the Old English style, then fashionable. The walls were painted or papered violet and Prince Albert arranged for the Regency profusion of pictures to be simplified. In 1914, during the reign of her husband George V, Queen Mary had the whole roof replaced and her chosen architect, Aston Webb, added the genteel garlands above the frieze. In 1931, the last traces of confident, quirky, Regency taste were swept away when the boldly sculpted surrounds to the two central doorways were replaced with more swags of fruit and flowers. The four Italian-carved fireplaces alone survive of the original decorative scheme (the medallion portraits on them are of Van Dyck, Dürer, Titian and Leonardo da Vinci).

The furniture here is French and the pedestals supporting bronze busts of two Emperors once stood in Louis XV's bedroom at Versailles.

In the lobby of the Gallery the sculpted figures of a woman and two children are those of Mrs Jordan, an actress, and two of her many illegitimate offspring. The work was commissioned by William IV, for she had been his mistress when he was the impoverished Duke of Clarence and the children, presumably, were his too. The portrait of Mrs Jordan was made after her death and the likeness may not be a good one. It is a touching reminder of his fondness for her, although he perhaps also felt guilty about turning her out of his house and marrying Princess Adelaide.

Milkmaids with Cattle in a Landscape: The Farm at Laeken by Sir Peter Paul Rubens (c 1617)

The Shipbuilder and His Wife – Rembrandt, 1633

The Rape of Europa – Claude Lorrain, 1677

THE *Picture* GALLERY

Although works acquired by earlier monarchs are shown here, it is once again principally George IV's taste and good fortune (he bought *The Rape of Europa*, one of the most sublime Claudes, for only £2,100) that is displayed here. In the 18th century it was felt that Dutch and Flemish paintings of the previous century were the ideal partners for contemporary *objets d'art* and furniture. As Prince Regent and King, George collected avidly, adding great existing collections like the Baring pictures and picking and choosing individual works in the salerooms and from his friends. There are 44 paintings shown at present of which the outstanding works are:

Cleopatra – Guido Reni (c1630)

The Libyan Sibyl – Guercino (c1651)

Interior of a Tavern with Cardplayers and a Viola Player – Jan Steen (c1665)

The Passage Boat – Aelbert Cuyp (c1650)

Christ and the Magdalen at the Tomb: 'Noli Me Tangere' – Rembrandt van Rijn (1638)

Portrait of a Man – Frans Hals (1630)

The Shipbuilder and His Wife – Rembrandt van Rijn (1633)

Agatha Bas – Rembrandt van Rijn (1641)

The Assumption of the Virgin – Sir Peter Paul Rubens (c1611)

The Mystic Marriage of St Catherine – Sir Anthony van Dyck (c1630)

Milkmaids with Cattle in a Landscape: 'The Farm at Laeken' – Sir Peter Paul Rubens (c1617-18)

A Courtyard in Delft at Evening: a Woman Spinning – Pieter de Hooch (c1657)

A Calm: A States Yacht under Sail, close to the Shore, and many other Vessels – Willem van de Velde (c1655)

Charles I and Henrietta Maria with their two Eldest Children, 'The Greate Peece' (sic) – Sir Anthony van Dyck (c1632)

Landscape with St George and the Dragon – Sir Peter Paul Rubens (c1630)

The Rape of Europa – Claude Lorrain (1667)

Charles I with M de St Antoine – Sir Anthony van Dyck (1633)

Landscape with a Negro Page – Aelbert Cuyp (c1655)

THE _SILK_ TAPESTRY ROOM

The anteroom which connects the East Gallery with the Picture Gallery was known as the Wilkie Room when four pictures by Sir David Wilkie hung there. Those are now gone, as are the four panels of Italian needlework which gave the room its modern name and which depicted 'The Adoration of the Magi', 'The Death of the First Born', 'The Flight into Egypt' and 'Christ in the House of Simon the Leper'.

The principal interest of the room now lies in its furniture, but first, Allan Ramsay's _Queen Charlotte with her two Eldest Children_ (1764) deserves attention. It was deliberately related to van Dyck's group portrait of Charles I, Henrietta Maria and their two eldest children (hanging in the Picture Gallery). As King George III's portraitist, Ramsay often painted his Queen and never better than this.

The two other pictures are _The Finding of Moses_ by Francesco Zuccarelli (1768) and Benjamin West's _The Apotheosis of Prince Octavius_ (1783).

The most striking piece of furniture is the side-table veneered with ebony and fitted with panels of pietra dura (semi-precious stones) which probably dates from the late 17th century and is stamped by Adam Weisweiler. The mahogany-veneered French chest of drawers is also attributed to him. On it stands three Chinese vases in mazarine blue with French rococo ormolu mounts in the Louis XV and Louis XVI styles.

The clocks are both French, the one with the carved figures is said to have been won in a wager by George IV from King Charles X of France.

Another King of France is recalled in the sculpture which is a reduction of E Bouchardon's equestrian statue of Louis XV which was unveiled in the Place de la Concorde in 1763. This copy was made a year later.

THE
EAST
GALLERY

The East Gallery, formerly known as the Promenade Gallery, connects the Ballroom with the Grand Staircase and the Supper Room. So its first function was to allow large numbers of people, some of whom would have been dressed in the great hooped skirts of the mid-Victorian period, to move with ease from one place to the other.

The Gallery was completed in 1855. It is about 6 metres (20ft) wide and as long as a terrace of six or seven small London houses, but James Pennethorne (the architect) proportioned it so well that it does not seem uncomfortably large. Pennethorne used the same door designs that his uncle, John Nash, had used in the earlier State Apartments. Pennethorne was a great exponent of pastiche and was adept at making his decorations sympathetic to the earlier style. As in other parts of the Palace the originally marbled walls have since been obliterated. Perhaps it is to the good if they coloured the light in which the pictures are seen, yet it is disappointing not to see the painted alcoves containing urns of cascading flowers that were once here.

Only an expert eye will notice that money was saved on the ornamental details which here are of cheaper 'composition', not ormolu (British monarchs have frequently, throughout history, needed to make economies). The coved glass roof, copied later by Aston Webb in the main Picture Gallery, serves the room's daytime function – displaying more of the Royal Collection paintings in a clear light. Beneath it is a frieze of 16 rectangular panels in grisaille, a monochrome technique intended to look like sculpted relief. They are by Nichola Consoni, an artist admired by Prince Albert, and they depict 'Cupids at Play' (perhaps a reference to the couples on their way to the Ballroom?).

The family of Queen Victoria and Prince Albert by Winterhalter was painted in 1846 when their children numbered five. Four more were to follow

Detail from West's portrait of George III, which shows the King as a military leader

THE ℰAST GALLERY

The Gallery houses a great pedestal clock, fully 2.8 metres (9ft) high, which came from Versailles to Carlton House, the former home of King George IV, in 1816. Although stamped by the cabinet-maker François Duhamel, experts believe that it was probably made in the 1730s, 20 years before he was active. The case is inlaid with veneers of tulipwood, rosewood and kingwood, superbly mounted in chased ormolu.

There are 11 paintings in this room. To the left are:

The Family of Balthasar Gerbier – Sir Peter Paul Rubens (c1630)

George IV – John Russell (1791). Painted when George was Prince of Wales, he is shown in the uniform of the Royal Kentish Bowmen.

The Family of Queen Victoria – Franz Xavier Winterhalter (1846). The chairs from the Green Drawing Room may be recognised.

George IV – John Hoppner (1796). Also painted when he was the Prince of Wales.

To the right are:

Queen Charlotte – Benjamin West (1782). This was a favourite picture of King George III. Thirteen of his children are shown, all of whom, save the eldest, were born in the Queen's House (now Buckingham Palace).

Prince Adolphus – Benjamin West (1778). Adolphus, sixth son of George III and later Duke of Cambridge is shown with Princess Mary and Princess Sophia.

George III – Benjamin West (1779). King George V commanded that all the West portraits of George III and his family should be brought here from Kensington Palace in 1915.

Francis, 5th Duke of Bedford – John Hoppner (c1797)

The Coronation of Queen Victoria – Sir George Hayter (1838)

Francis, 5th Earl of Moira – John Hoppner (c1793)

Frederick, Duke of York – Sir Joshua Reynolds (1787-88). Second son of George III.

Queen Charlotte and her family of 13 children by Benjamin West, left

Right, the monumental pedestal clock, over 250 years old

43

THE *C*ROSS AND *W*EST GALLERIES

In 1853 James Pennethorne designed for Queen Victoria a ballroom, the State or Ball Supper Room, the East and West Galleries, and the small Cross Gallery which connects them. In the Cross Gallery hang two paintings by Benjamin West which once graced the Warm Room at Buckingham House before its transformation by George IV. To the left is *The Departure of Regulus from Rome* (pictured), to the right is *The Oath of Hannibal*, which depicts him swearing never to make peace with Rome.

The West Gallery is less than a third of the length of the East Gallery to which it lies parallel. It used to be called the Approach Gallery and it is here that the orchestra plays during State Dinners. On its walls hang four Gobelin tapestries, each 3 metres (10ft) square, enlivened with scenes from Don Quixote. They were designed by Charles Antoine Coypel and were woven in the 1700s by Neilson, who invented the *rose damassée* (pink damask) ground. The subjects are: 'Don Quixote cured by Wisdom of his Madness'; 'The awakening of Sancho and his despair at the loss of his ass'; 'Sancho administering justice in Batavia'; and 'The Princess begging Don Quixote to restore her to her throne'. Above the doorways at either end are life-size groups in high relief by William Theed the Younger, a popular sculptor of the day. They represent 'Venus Descending with the Armour of Achilles' and 'The Birth of Venus'.

THE $\mathscr{S}$TATE DINING ROOM

This is the last room in the enfilade (or series of rooms arranged to form a processional route) which started at the White Drawing Room. There are places for up to 60 guests to join the Queen and HRH The Duke of Edinburgh at the great Spanish mahogany table in the State Dining Room. It is used for formal meals that are not quite as grand as State Banquets, such as those given when Heads of Government meet in London for a summit, or the King's Derby Day Dinners, which King Edward VII and King George V used to give for the Jockey Club.

It was at the south-west corner of Nash's original palace, yet in many ways the room is not really his. When Nash was sacked in 1830 for over-running his budget the interior had hardly been begun and the new chosen architect, Edward Blore, discarded Nash's design in favour of a grander scheme. He still retained the mirror doors which Nash had introduced and the curved shutter cases and parquetry floor are like those of the first State Apartments.

The room was not finished until after King William IV's death and the cypher of his successor, Queen Victoria, appears in many of the ornamental medallions. The State Dining Room was conceived by a man of the Regency taste and delivered by Victorians and it shows. The three-domed ceiling, heavily encrusted with gold, may look to the inexpert eye like the works of John Nash, but it has been criticised by Dr Pevsner, the architectural historian, for the 'heavy and restless bracketing of the cove', a motif he says Nash would have disdained.

There is perhaps a hint of a less refined taste too in the four heavily-gilted chandeliers; but then taste, as Buckingham Palace constantly reminds its visitors, is a shifting sand.

*The portraits of Queen Charlotte and
King George III (far right)
may be forerunners of our royal
souvenirs - 90 copies of this pair were
produced for sale to loyal subjects*

*The life-size portrait of King George IV
in his Coronation robes*

*Frederick, Prince of Wales
by Van Loo: Frederick is the same
prince who drew such indifference from
his mother, Queen Caroline*

THE *S*TATE DINING ROOM

Along one wall of the State Dining Room are some of the most regal of the royal portraits, gazing majestically down on the diners. They are interesting for the way in which the displays illustrate the development of state portraiture during the second half of the 18th century.

The life-size portrait of King George IV over the mantelpiece was painted around 1820. (Confidently described for generations as being by Sir Thomas Lawrence, modern scholarship now prefers to say that it is by his 'studio'.) The King's hand rests on the Sèvres table which Louis XVIII had given to him (now in the Blue Drawing Room next door). On the table too is St Edward's Crown, named after the Saxon king and saint, but made in 1660 for King Charles II. This is the crown with which Elizabeth II was crowned Queen in 1953.

To either side of the Lawrence painting are Allan Ramsay's portraits of *King George III* and *Queen Charlotte* in their Coronation robes. Ramsay and his studio produced about 90 pairs of copies of the Coronation portraits which were sent to Ambassadors and Governors of Provinces, and might be bought by loyal subjects from the Lord Chamberlain's Department. This Queen Charlotte could be such a copy.

The marble and gilt bronze clock with three figures in Derby 'biscuit' china representing astronomy, a child, and an angel, was made in 1788 by Benjamin Vulliamy. William Duesbury made the porcelain figures. The second clock represents Apollo in his chariot, drawn by four horses.

The four five-light candelabra on red marble bases by F Redmond were made for a closet decorated in 'the Turkish taste' in the apartments of the Comte d'Artois at Versailles.

THE $\mathcal{B}$LUE DRAWING ROOM

Nash designed this room in the mid-1820s as the ballroom of the Palace. The exuberant spirit of its decoration recalls the preceding decade, when dancing the waltz was new and sensational. Pattern, rhythm and balance, characteristics of both dance and architecture, are enhanced by lovely colouring. Corinthian capitals top 30 columns in pairs that were to be of rose-coloured scagliola, but were soon painted to represent onyx. Four immensely long chandeliers glitter just above the dancers' heads. But the party spirit is curbed by the classical discipline with which Nash proportioned the long room. The columns stand almost clear of the walls so they catch the light from the west-facing windows and cast modelling shadows. The entablature (architrave, frieze and cornice) pushes out into the room above them to support great trusses. These curve over the coffered sides of the richly-carved ceiling to support shallow saucer domes.

The name of the room comes from the flock wallpaper of a turquoise colour on an umber background, the blue satin brocade of the curtains, pelmets and coverings of the exquisite gilt chairs. The Axminster carpet (replaced during public opening) repeats the same blue interwoven into its pattern of red and gold. The space is divided into two unequal parts: an anteroom, slightly lower, is separated from the three-bayed ceiling of the larger part by a lintel. Above the very richly gilded entablature here and at either end of the room are emblematic groups of figures in high relief by William Pitts representing Shakespeare, Milton and Spencer on Mount Parnassus – curiously reflective subjects for a ballroom, but they were not put in place until 1836 and although this remained the Ballroom until 1854, a more earnest mood had by then come over the Palace.

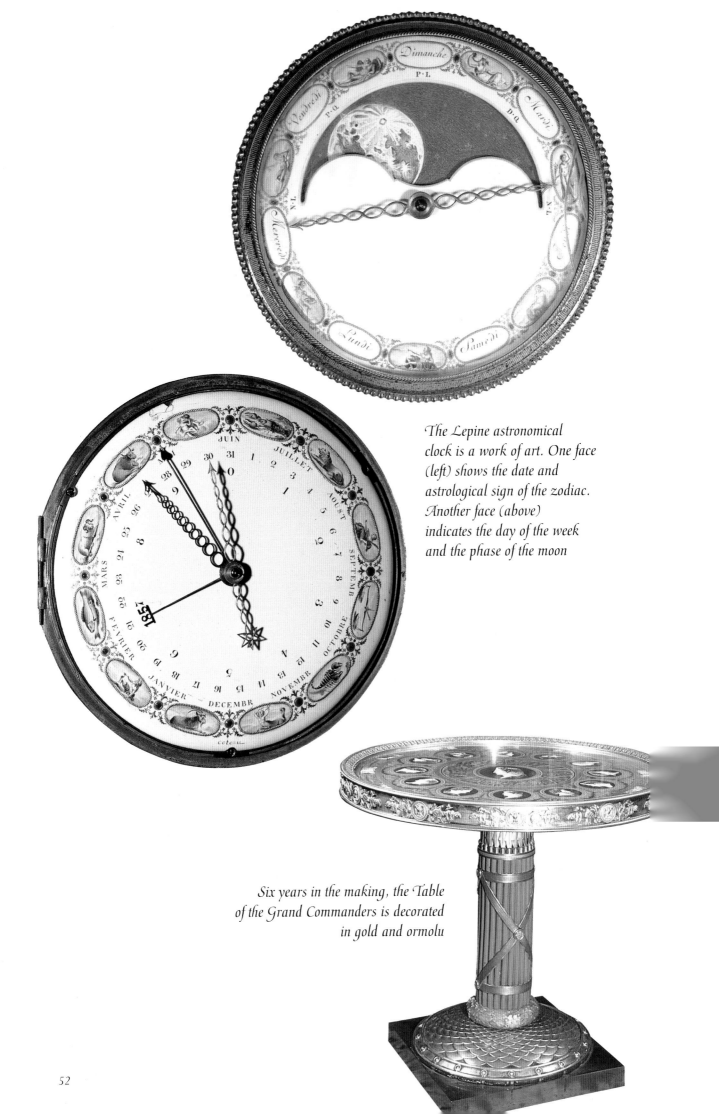

The Lepine astronomical
clock is a work of art. One face
(left) shows the date and
astrological sign of the zodiac.
Another face (above)
indicates the day of the week
and the phase of the moon

Six years in the making, the Table
of the Grand Commanders is decorated
in gold and ormolu

THE $\mathscr{B}$LUE DRAWING ROOM

Among the noteworthy works in this room is the Table of the Grand Commanders. Napoleon Bonaparte ordered this extraordinary piece of furniture in 1806. It is made of hard-paste Sèvres porcelain and took six years to complete. After Napoleon's defeat, it was given to King George IV by the restored King of France and it soon became one of the King's favourite possessions, so much so that he instructed court painter Sir Thomas Lawrence to include it in all official portraits (one version can be seen in the State Dining Room). The table-top (which revolves) is painted with the head of Alexander the Great and twelve great commanders of antiquity, all in imitation of cameo reliefs. Beneath the portraits are scenes from each of their lives. The decorations are in gold and ormolu, symbolic of Roman and French military glory, and the whole is set on a column of Roman fasces (the bundled rods of authority) and a plinth in the form of a shield.

The State Portrait of the Queen's grandfather King George V is by Sir Luke Fildes who had painted Queen Mary before she married the King. The painting of her in this room, however, is by Sir William Llewellyn.

The beautiful clock which immediately commands attention in this room is one of great importance. It is an astronomical clock and is by the clockmaker to Louis XV, Jean Antoine Lepine. It has been called his masterpiece. It was bought by the Prince Regent in 1790 and, apart from the time of day, it tells the days of the month and week, the phases of the moon and the astrological sign appropriate to the date.

The other pieces of furniture in the room were acquired by George IV for the Royal residences of Windsor Castle and Carlton House, as were the pairs of gilt bronze candelabra incorporating a flaming torch and chains hung from eagles' heads.

George V by Sir Luke Fildes

THE

$\mathcal{M}$USIC ROOM

This room acquired its name from the early piano which used to stand in the bay. It was originally the Bow State Drawing Room and here the Sovereign's guests, having assembled in the Green Drawing Room, are presented before processing through to the Ballroom or State Dining Room. The Prince of Wales, born in the Palace on 14 November 1948, was brought here in the lace and satin robe worn by Queen Victoria's children, to be baptised; the Private Chapel where the Queen was christened in 1926 having been destroyed by enemy action during the war. Thus another Royal tradition began. Nash uses the same style of columns here as in the Blue Drawing Room next door, but this time they are made in deep blue scagliola in imitation of lapis lazuli. The ceiling is deeply domed, and between cornice and dome are relief panels by William Pitts representing Harmony, Eloquence and Pleasure. There is a clue here to Nash's intentions, for Harmony is over the door to the White Drawing Room, once intended as a music room.

Suspended from the centre of the dome and from the half-dome of the bay are two huge chandeliers – perhaps the most magnificent in the Palace. Today, the warm, inconstant light from the 112 candles which used to burn in the chandeliers for state occasions has been replaced by the safer and duller electric sort.

The small armchairs and settees were made in France about 1786 by the celebrated cabinet-maker Georges Jacob. They were obtained from the highly fashionable shop of Dominique Daguerre, a dealer who fled from Paris when Louis XVI was executed and set up in Sloane Street, where the Prince Regent ran up a bill of £15,000.

The satinwood and white holly floor is inlaid with medallions at each corner bearing the cypher of George IV.

THE *W*HITE DRAWING ROOM

The western range of State Rooms begins with the Royal Closet, where the Royal Family assembles privately before formal processions to state events. The Royal party enjoys a little drama on these occasions: they join those waiting in the glittering White Drawing Room through a surprising concealed door, a huge mirror with an ebony cabinet fixed in front of it, all of which swings open to allow them through. The room into which they pass overlooks the calm vista of the gardens through three tall windows framed with solid mahogany shutters which match those in the other two rooms of the suite beyond.

The central dished panels of the ceiling also match those of the Blue Drawing Room, but now John Nash springs his surprises. For the plump columns to which we have become accustomed are here replaced by pilasters (once of yellow scagliola, painted white in 1873) pressed flat against the wall and the capitals, in other rooms usually pure Corinthian, are here a composite of his devising incorporating the Star and Garter.

The white and gold of this room is strongly reminiscent of the Edwardian era, but it is not. Originally the room contained more yellow and was darker in appearance. The pier-glasses (the tall mirrors with Baroque decoration) were added to the room by Edward Blore but the room is still essentially Nash.

The second surprise he produces in this room is in the treatment of the ceiling, the coving of which is made convex in a way that suggests tented drapery. Beneath it, 12 panels in relief run right round the room. They are by the seemingly ubiquitous William Pitts and are fantastic allegories on 'the Origin and Progress of Pleasure', an appropriate theme for the former Prince Regent, who died shortly before they were finished.

*The finely-detailed inlay in many woods
on this roll-top desk is believed to be the
work of Riesener*

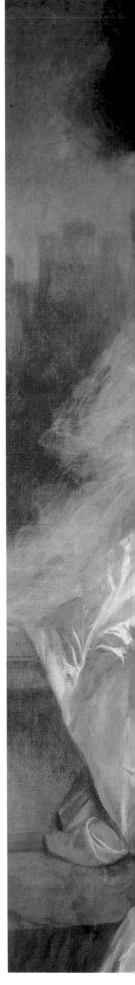

*One of Britain's best-loved
consorts, Queen Alexandra is captured
in this portrait by Flameng*

THE *W*HITE DRAWING ROOM

This most impressive room draws light and majesty from the gold upholstery and heavy curtains. Overlooking the whole is a portrait of Queen Alexandra, wife of Edward VII, painted in 1908 by François Flameng. Queen Alexandra, the Queen's great-grandmother, was the daughter of King Christian IX of Denmark. She married at eighteen and although the marriage was arranged, she declared: "You may think I am marrying Bertie for his position; but if he were a cowboy I would love him just the same." Her good nature, which equalled her great beauty and high spirits, was often tried and never found wanting.

Bought at auction in 1825 from a West Indies landowner who had fallen on hard times, the superb desk by Jean-Henri Riesener was intended by King George IV for Windsor Castle. It was made around 1775 in Paris. It is of oak veneered with purplewood, bois-satiné, casuarina wood, holly, box, sycamore and other woods in part stained and engraved. The attribution to Riesener is based on the similarities in the inlays to other desks at Versailles which the maître-ébéniste signed; for example the emblems of Poetry and Literature. Typical too is the 'central locking' mechanism which ensures that the principal drawers are locked when the roll top is closed. The desk has a secret compartment and may have originally been made for one of Louis XV's daughters.

The candelabra of gilt and patinated bronze are late 18th-century French. The finely-modelled figures of Nymphs and Fauns bearing cornucopias are perhaps by the sculptor Etienne-Maurice Falconet. They stand on gilded wooden pedestals supported by three cranes, made in 1811 for Carlton House.

The piano in a gilded case made by S and P Erard is painted in polychrome colours and was bought by Queen Victoria in 1856.

THE $\mathcal{M}$INISTERS' STAIRCASE

Leading down from the White Drawing Room and the State Apartments at the north end of the Palace is Edward Blore's Ministers' Staircase. It gives access to the Marble Hall and the ground floor Apartments and was built in 1834. On its walls hang two large Gobelins tapestries which were woven in the 1750s and designed by J M Viens. They depict the mythological rapes of Europa and Proserpine and belong to a set of four, *Les Amours des Dieux*. The tapestries were bought by George IV in 1826.

A great clock and barograph, no less than 2.8 metres (9ft 4in) high, stands at the stairhead. It was made in 1765 by Alexander Cumming, a Scot, for King George III. The king's precise, regular nature loved horology and he could, with his own hands, dismantle and reassemble the most complicated watches. His interest in clocks and barometers laid the foundations of the Royal Collection of some 300 clocks. He liked English instruments while his son, King George IV, added to the collection the many fine French clocks which he preferred.

This clock/barograph (a detail from its face is pictured on the left) has an escapement designed by Cumming and a compensation pendulum by the King's clockmaker, John Ellicott, a Fellow of the Royal Society. In the centre of the dial hours, minutes and seconds are shown more or less conventionally. Around it are two annular dial bands which record the weather for every day throughout the year by pencil on the vellum of the dials. A system of ivory rods and carriages transmits the varying data from the barometer beneath, while actual barometric height is indicated on a pointer driven by a cord from the float. As well as paying Cumming £1,178 for making the clock, King George wisely gave him an annual allowance of £150 for keeping it in order.

THE ${\mathcal{M}}$ARBLE HALL

In a palace of long corridors, the 60 metre-long (200 ft) Marble Hall is by no means the longest. It runs from the foot of the Ministers' Staircase back past the Great Hall, almost to the southernmost end of the building and it fills the space occupied by the garden rooms in old Buckingham House: Nash, asked by his Royal client to improve an existing house rather than build a new palace, worked as far as possible within the existing walls.

The Marble Hall follows the route the Duke of Buckingham took to his 'little closet of books' and the greenhouse in which he sat listening to the nightingales in his 'wilderness'. These rooms later became George III's private apartments (Queen Charlotte's were upstairs), convenient for his voluminous libraries.

This Hall is the last stage in the gradual process which turned a small country house into an Imperial palace. Like the Great Hall, it is nobly lined with paired Corinthian columns of Ravacconi marble and paved with an inlaid marble floor. The deep frieze is decorated with swagged garlands, rosettes and leaves (faintly reminiscent of the Prince of Wales's feathers) on a trellis of tilted squares, all gilt. The modillions (brackets in the angle between ceiling and wall) are richly gilt too, and the ceiling is panelled and enriched. Yet this sumptuous decoration was not enough for the Edwardian taste. Perhaps Nash himself would have found the walls too blank once the coloured scagliola had gone. But in 1903 the firm of Bertram & Son, working under Frank Verity, was employed to add the trophies of musical instruments and festoons of fruit and flowers in carved and gilded wood. Although well enough done, Bertram was not Grinling Gibbons, and the work adds little to a fine passage.

Winterhalter's portrait of Queen Victoria at the age of 40, when she had ruled Britain and the Empire for 22 years

Classic lines and cool eroticism distinguish Antonio Canova's Fountain Nymph with Putto

THE *M*ARBLE HALL

The walls of the Marble Hall are lined with noble portraits, but two particularly fine pieces of sculpture demand attention first. Antonio Canova was the most successful sculptor of his day, and visited London in 1815. King George IV already knew and admired his work. He had bought a nude statue of Napoleon (which the Emperor hated) and generously gave it to the Duke of Wellington for Apsley House. Now, following Canova's visit, he commissioned the sculptor to make *Mars and Venus*. It was delivered nine years later but in the meantime King George had persuaded Lord Cawdor to let him have the *Fountain Nymph with Putto* (naked child), which the nobleman had ordered. Neo-classical sculptors all aspired towards 'noble simplicity and serene grandeur' and Canova's brilliant technique, supported by fine life drawing and tinged with cool eroticism, allowed him to achieve these qualities.

The official portraits of *Queen Victoria and Prince Albert, Prince Consort* are by Franz Xavier Winterhalter and were painted in 1859. In the Queen's portrait can be seen the distant outline of Charles Barry's new Houses of Parliament in the Palace of Westminster, which would not be complete until the following year. Prince Albert is in the dark green uniform of Colonel of the Rifle Brigade.

The other portraits in the Marble Hall are likenesses of the Royal couple's relatives: Victoria's uncle, *Augustus, Duke of Sussex* (Domenico Pellegrini, c1803); *Victoire, Duchess of Nemours,* cousin of Queen Victoria (Winterhalter 1849); *Ernest I, Duke of Saxe-Coburg-Gotha,* the Prince Consort's father (George Dawe c1818); and *Victoria, Duchess of Kent*, Queen Victoria's mother (Winterhalter 1849).

Canova's Mars and Venus, commissioned by George IV, one of Buckingham Palace's most avid collectors

THE BOW ROOM

Immediately under the Music Room, on the central axis of the west front facing the gardens, is the Bow Room. Familiar to those large numbers of people invited every year to the Royal Garden Parties, it gives direct access to the Terrace. It has also been known in the past as the Bow Library, or the 1853 Room, after the date upon its frieze.

Unlike the lofty Music Room above it, the Bow Room is restricted to the height of the ground floor rooms of the old Buckingham House. Nash dug out the Great Hall to create extra height but here the low, flat ceiling rather depresses the proportions of the room. Nash did his best to lighten our spirits, however. He cleverly placed his columns to form two alcoves and in two of the corners placed curved, glazed, display cabinets for porcelain.

The black marble chimney-pieces with burnished 'sarcophagus' grates on either side of the doorway into the Marble Hall are contemporary with the room. They were commissioned by the Earl of Bridgewater from Benjamin Louis Vulliamy, son and grandson of the celebrated Royal clockmakers. The chimney-pieces were first installed at 7 Grosvenor Square. Later they went to Lord Farquhar's house at Castle Rising in Norfolk, from where Queen Mary, wife of George V and grandmother of our present Queen, brought them in the 1920s.

Compared to the ornate rooms above, the Bow Room is simple and workaday. Ionic capitals topping the columns replace the more decorative orders upstairs and white paint covers the walls, but the gilt detailing and the rich crimson of the carpet, the curtains and the upholstery invest the relative simplicity with a still palatial grandeur.

The Chelsea service known as the
Mecklenburg-Strelitz service
after Duke Adolphus Frederick IV to
whom it was given

Despite the room's comparative simplicity, it too contains some remarkable pieces. The foremost of these must be the Chelsea service, one of the finest examples of tableware in the English rococo style, which was given by King George III (who had commissioned it) to his wife Queen Charlotte's brother, Duke Adolphus Frederick IV of Mecklenburg-Strelitz. It was made in 1763. The material is soft-paste bone-ash porcelain; the decoration is in underglaze mazarine blue, with enamel colours and gilding. The service was brought from Germany in 1919 by Sir Joseph Duveen and it returned to the British Royal Family in 1947 when it was presented to Her Majesty Queen Elizabeth the Queen Mother by James Oakes, Esq.

The inkstands atop more recent tables in the window bays are a pair of Regency kingwood and gilt bronze pieces, fitted with richly chased candlesticks with reversible nozzles. The (slightly) finer of the two was used by King George IV in the King's Closet at Carlton House.

The object resembling a mahogany-covered urn on a pedestal is a late 18th-century, English-made incense burner and was one of a pair bought by Queen Mary.

The portraits were set into the panelling at the request of Queen Victoria. They show the Royal family's extensive links with the Royal families of Europe. On the left are Marie Henriette, Queen of the Belgians (1854); Ferdinand of Savoy, Duke of Genoa (1853); Augusta, Princess of Prussia, later Queen of Prussia and German Empress (1853); Ernest, Prince of Hohenlohe-Langenburg (1853); Prince Leopold, later Duke of Albany (1853); Leopold II, King of the Belgians. On the right are: George V of Hanover (1853); Frederick William, Grand Duke of Mecklenburg-Strelitz (1853); Princess Augusta of Cambridge, Grand Duchess of Mecklenburg-Strelitz (1853); George, Duke of Cambridge (1852); Princess Mary Adelaide of Cambridge (1847); and Maria Alexandrina, Queen of Hanover (1853).

THE TERRACE & GARDENS

At the end of the 18th century, fashionable garden designers, notably William Townsend Aiton, popularised in England the idea of separating the house from the garden by a terrace. Ladies in long dresses appreciated the paved or gravelled surface underfoot; their gardeners enjoyed the opportunity offered by the stone vases usually set into the balustrade to display the new bedding plants; a gentleman's taste in fashionably antique sculpture looked well upon it; and everyone found the elevated terrace the best place from which to admire the vistas provided by the landscape designer.

Aiton worked with John Nash on the gardens of the Brighton Pavilion, on Regent's Park, Carlton House and Royal Lodge at Windsor. At Windsor Castle, he had used the terrace beneath the King's private apartments as a vantage point from which to enjoy the pattern of a very formal garden like the parterres of old, with box hedges clipped into geometrical shapes and gravel walks between. At Buckingham Palace the garden was to be more in the 'picturesque' style, mimicking the parkland surrounding country houses. There were to be no formal patterns near the house: instead, the King wanted a large lawn on which to entertain and that is what he got.

The enormous lawn was intended for garden fêtes (the meaning has changed greatly since Prince Regent's day). At Carlton House the Prince had entertained lavishly, instructing Nash to build fantastic temporary pavilions for his guests. It was not until Queen Victoria started the Royal Garden Parties that the garden and terrace were used for entertaining as they are today. Now, at four o'clock on the days of the Garden Parties, the Queen's group descends the steps and joins her 10,000 guests on the grass and chamomile turf. The Terrace then becomes a broad line drawn between formality and informality, between Palace and garden, between Court and people.

King George IV was clear about what he wanted in the spacious grounds of Buckingham Palace; privacy, good views, particularly of the Palace itself for he was greatly

Up to 10,000 invited guests throng one of the summer Garden Parties

The Queen's party descends to join Garden Party guests

The West Front of Buckingham Palace viewed from across the lake with its flock of flamingos

pleased with it, and he wanted space on which to entertain.

First a three-and-a-half acre lake was dug and the spoil was used to make a mound to hide the palace stables. Around the perimeter of the 39-acre garden a high wall was built and within it other mounds were raised, picturesque hillocks that helped hide the surrounding houses of Belgravia, which was then being rapidly developed. Many trees were planted as screens.

For years there was difficulty feeding the lake. In 1883 the gardeners complained that its fetid water was so disgusting that they would not work nearby in summer. A new, clean source was found in a well on Duck Island in St James's Park. Flamingos now totter in the shallows and look for the roach, perch, gudgeon the lake contains.

Long after Victorian times, the London air, heavily polluted with sulphurous coal smuts, made gardening difficult. Since the Clean Air Acts were introduced in the 1950s, the sooty old evergreen shrubberies have been steadily replaced with more sensitive and attractive planting and the tired soil has been enriched or replaced. The Royal Mews is a continuing source of that commodity priceless to gardeners, 'well-rotted farmyard manure'.

Two-and-a-half miles of gravelled paths were made to Aiton's ground-plan and they have been little altered since. Trees were planted to give walkers seclusion and to provide a frame through which to view the west side of the Palace. Recently, cunning planting has shielded the Queen and her family from intrusive eyes in the modern buildings rising above the old trees. The laburnum tunnel and an avenue of Indian chestnuts, planted in 1961 along the Conservatory Walk, are such innovations.

The space King George IV wanted is provided by the huge lawn on which the feet of countless garden-party guests have trampled and where the helicopters of the Royal Flight now land. To the summer guests the great herbaceous border, 158 metres (520 ft) long, is the principal horticultural attraction. If they wander far enough from the tea tent they may find the enormous Waterloo Vase, 4.5 metres (15 ft) high and carved from a single stone or the charming Garden House made around 1730. In the Spring bloom tens of thousands of crocuses, *Iris reticulata*, snowdrops, scillas, chionodoxas, winter aconites, fritillaries and narcissi which have been planted during the Queen's reign. Even in winter it is truly a magnificent garden, worthy of a Royal Palace.

THE *Q*UEEN'S GALLERY

In September 1940, at the height of the Battle of Britain, a German bomb fell on the Private Chapel at Buckingham Palace and destroyed it. However, the site of the chapel provided an ideal place on which to construct a small art gallery which would be conveniently accessible to the public and in 1962 the Queen's Gallery, as it is known, opened with an exhibition called *Treasures from The Royal Collection*. It was also the first time that members of the public had been able to enter a part of Buckingham Palace.

The collection from which the Gallery has drawn its 26 subsequent exhibitions is unique. It is the largest private holding of art in the world, but that would be of little account if it were not also one of the finest. It has variety and magnificence; universally known masterpieces and obscure works treasured only by scholars; it mainly reflects European taste of the past three centuries, but it also has good examples of Asian, American and Australasian art. And it has the additional interest of having been made by our kings and queens – real people with strong views about art: some connoisseurs, some with an astute financial eye.

The scholars and technicians who look after the Royal Collection are computerising their inventory of the holdings. Their task is enormous. Seven thousand paintings (three times the number in the National Gallery), 1,400 pieces of sculpture, 30,000 drawings and watercolours, over 2,000 miniatures and about 500,000 prints are to be listed and described. They have been assembled from around the world: purchases, gifts and commissions.

And then there is the furniture, glass, porcelain, arms and armour, textiles, silver, gold and jewellery, including the Crown Jewels, perhaps a million objects in all, no one is yet quite sure. To value it is impossible, but anyone

Canaletto's The Grand Canal from the Carita towards the Bacind

Below, Self-Portrait as an old Woman, by Rosalba Carriera

Right, The Adoration of the Magi, by Sebastiano Ricci

trying to assemble such a collection today would need not millions but billions of pounds.

They would have to find one of the finest of all Vermeers (The Music Lesson), several magnificent Rembrandts, important paintings by Claude, van Dyck, Rubens, Breugel, Raphael, Giovanni Bellini, Tintoretto, Fra Angelico, Duccio, Cranach, Dürer, Holbein and many works by other artists of greater or lesser distinction.

This mega-millionaire would have to look for drawings by Leonardo and Michelangelo (of which the Royal Collection holds hundreds of the finest examples) before widening the holding with works by a thousand other artists.

The finest Sèvres porcelain in the world, wonderful furniture, clocks and armour, bronzes, plate and glass, enough to furnish seven palaces, would each take a lifetime to collect; and the Crown Jewels and the royal portraits are not for sale.

How fortunate, then, that Her Majesty wishes that all these treasures, which she holds in trust for her successors, are to be publicly displayed as often as is practicable in her own Gallery, in her palaces and by loan elsewhere.

The tragic fire at Windsor Castle has brought some small consolation for lovers of art. At present, the Queen's Gallery is exhibiting *A King's Purchase*, consisting of the great collection made by George III, who bought Buckingham House, and who wished to obtain some paintings with which to decorate his new home. One of the astute buyers, rather than a connoisseur, his collection, which includes over 500 oils, is usually housed at Windsor and many of these works have never before been seen in London. The works illustrated here are from that collection.

The Queen's Gallery is open to the public six days of the week, between 10am and 5pm from Tuesday to Saturday and from 2pm to 5pm on Sundays. In addition it is open on Bank Holiday Mondays.

Portrait of a Young Man by Giovanni Bellini

THE $\mathcal{R}$OYAL MEWS

T he Royal Mews is an integral part of Buckingham Palace, located along the south side of the Palace. It provides the transport for the Queen whenever she begins a journey by road. It is a working department of the Royal Household, despite being open to visitors, and it houses the horses, carriages and limousines belonging to Her Majesty.

In the Middle Ages a mews was a place where the king's falcons were kept during their 'mewing', or change of plumage. For centuries the king's mews were located near Charing Cross, on the northern side of what is now Trafalgar Square. Until the reign of Henry VIII they housed only falcons, but a fire in 1537 destroyed the royal stables and the King ordered the stable to be moved to the Charing Cross mews and the falcons gave way to horses.

King George III made the decision to move some of his stud and carriage into the stables behind Buckingham House, which he had purchased in 1762. In 1824, four years after George IV had come to the throne, John Nash was commissioned to redesign the stables and coach-houses and they became the Royal Mews in 1825. This date can be seen on the weathercock above the stables.

Nash's design for the Mews is still evident today. Through a Doric arch one reaches the large Quadrangle around which the main coach-houses and stables are arranged. The State Stables, probably the finest in existence, are home to the 20 bay horses which are used every day and the 10 famous Windsor greys which draw the Queen's coach on ceremonial occasions.

There are seven of these carriages, housed on the

Above and below, the Glass Coach is driven in full regalia

The Australian State Coach, is used on the occasion of the State Opening of Parliament

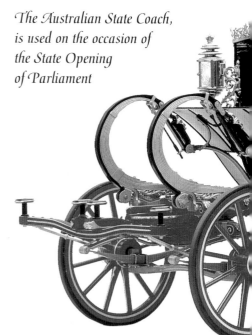

THE *Royal* MEWS

The Gold State Coach which dates
from 1762 and has been used for every Coronation
since that of George IV

*Immaculate
always,
the bay horses
which are
at work
every day*

eastern side of the Quadrangle, the most impressive of which is undoubtedly the Gold State Coach. This coach, which must surely be everyone's ideal of a Royal carriage, was first used on November 25, 1762 to convey George III to 'the House of Peers, to open the new session of Parliament'. It has been used for Coronations and great state occasions ever since, including the Coronation of Her Majesty Queen Elizabeth II in 1953. It was last used to convey the Queen to St Paul's Cathedral during the Silver Jubilee celebrations.

The carriage now used by the monarch to travel to the State Opening of Parliament each November is the newest of the State carriages, the Australian State Carriage. This was built and presented to the Queen during her tour of the country in 1988 to commemorate Australia's Bicentenary. It was first used by Her Majesty to attend the State Opening of Parliament in November 1988.

Reputedly the most comfortable of the major State Coaches is the Scottish State Coach, a favourite of Queen Elizabeth the Queen Mother, with its large windows and glass roof panels. Visitors to the Royal Mews are also able to see the beautiful Glass Coach, used by every Royal bride this century for the drive to her marriage.

The man in charge of the Royal Mews is the Crown Equerry, who makes all the necessary arrangements for the Queen to travel. The titular head of the Royal Mews is the Master of the Horse whose duties today are purely ceremonial. During State Processions he can be seen riding immediately behind the Queen.

In addition to the carriages and horses, the garages at the Royal Mews contain five Rolls-Royce limousines which are used to transport the Queen. The most famous of these is the Phantom VI presented to Her Majesty in 1978 by the Society of Motor Manufacturers and Traders to mark her Silver Jubilee.

THE *M*ONARCHS
OF ENGLAND *&* BRITAIN

Egbert (802-839)

Ethelwulf (839-855)

Ethelbald (855-860)

Ethelbert (860-866)

Ethelred (866-871)

Alfred the Great (871-899)

Edward the Elder (899-924)

Athelstan (924-940)

Edmund (940-946)

Edred (946-955)

Edwy (955-959)

Edgar (959-975)

Edward the Martyr (975-979)

Ethelred II, the Unready (979-1016)

Edmund Ironside (1016)

Canute (1016-1035)

Harthacanute and Harold I, jointly (1035)

Harold I, alone (1035-1040)

Harthacanute, again (1040-1042)

Edward the Confessor (1042-1066)

Harold II (1066)

William I, the Conqueror (1066-1087)

William II (1087-1100)

Henry I (1100-1135)

Stephen (1135-1154)

Henry II (1154-1189)

Richard I, the Lionheart (1189-1199)

John (1199-1216)

Henry III (1216-1272)

Edward I, Longshanks (1272-1307)

Edward II (1307-1327)

Edward III (1327-1377)

Richard II (1377-1399)

Henry IV (1399-1413)

Henry V (1413-1422)

Henry VI (1422-1461)

Edward IV (1461-1470)

Henry VI, again (1470-1471)

Edward IV, again (1471-1483)

Edward V (1483)

Richard III (1483-1485)

Henry VII (1485-1509)

Henry VIII (1509-1547)

Edward VI (1547-1553)

Mary I (1553-1558)

Elizabeth I (1558-1603)

James I (1603-1625)

Charles I (1625-1649)

Charles II (1660-1685)

James II (1685-1688)

William III (1680-1702) **& Mary II** (1689-1694)

Anne (1702-1714)

George I (1714-1727)

George II (1727-1760)

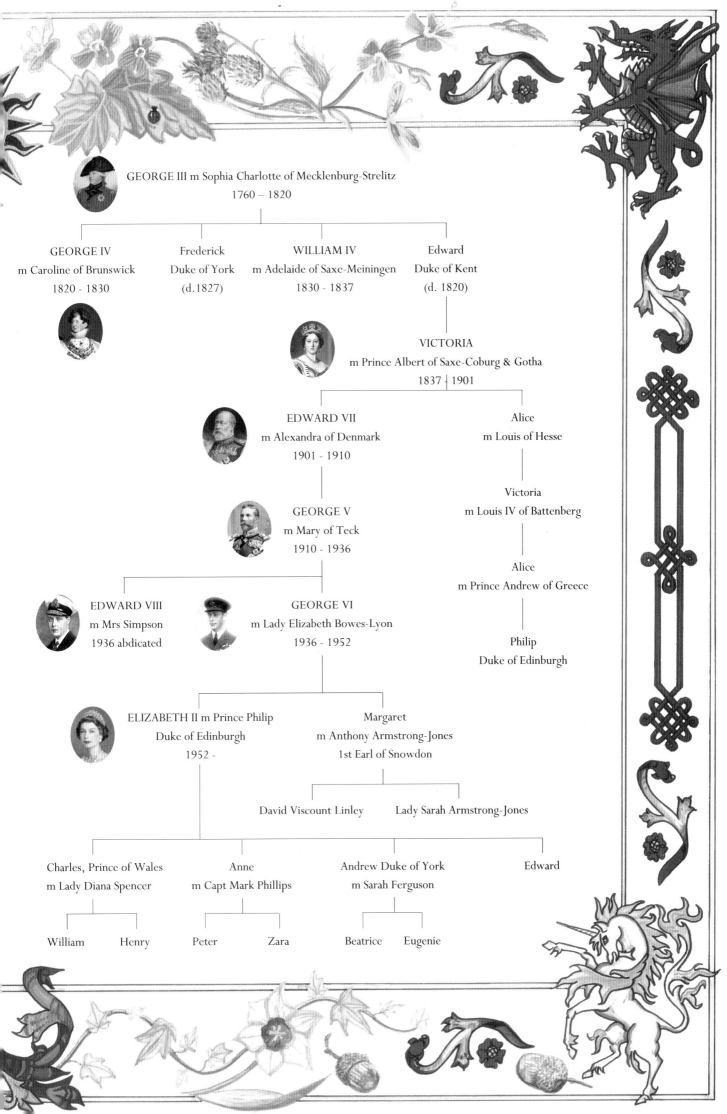

GEORGE III m Sophia Charlotte of Mecklenburg-Strelitz
1760 – 1820

GEORGE IV
m Caroline of Brunswick
1820 - 1830

Frederick
Duke of York
(d.1827)

WILLIAM IV
m Adelaide of Saxe-Meiningen
1830 - 1837

Edward
Duke of Kent
(d. 1820)

VICTORIA
m Prince Albert of Saxe-Coburg & Gotha
1837 - 1901

EDWARD VII
m Alexandra of Denmark
1901 - 1910

Alice
m Louis of Hesse

Victoria
m Louis IV of Battenberg

GEORGE V
m Mary of Teck
1910 - 1936

Alice
m Prince Andrew of Greece

EDWARD VIII
m Mrs Simpson
1936 abdicated

GEORGE VI
m Lady Elizabeth Bowes-Lyon
1936 - 1952

Philip
Duke of Edinburgh

ELIZABETH II m Prince Philip
Duke of Edinburgh
1952 -

Margaret
m Anthony Armstrong-Jones
1st Earl of Snowdon

David Viscount Linley

Lady Sarah Armstrong-Jones

Charles, Prince of Wales
m Lady Diana Spencer

Anne
m Capt Mark Phillips

Andrew Duke of York
m Sarah Ferguson

Edward

William

Henry

Peter

Zara

Beatrice

Eugenie

DIARY OF EVENTS

2 & 3 June

Beating Retreat: Household Division

Horse Guards Parade. A popular military display of marching drilling bands of the Household Division. Mounted bands, trumpeters, massed bands and pipe and drums. Performances are given at 9.30pm by floodlight. Tickets available from the end of February from: Premier Box Office, 1b Bridge Street, London SW1 (opposite Big Ben). Tel: 071-839 6815/6732.

12 June

The Queen's Birthday Parade – Trooping The Colour

The Queen leaves Buckingham Palace around 10.40am and goes down The Mall to Horse Guards Parade arriving at 11am. The National Anthem is played and a Gun Salute is fired in Green Park. After inspecting the parade, the Queen arrives back at the Palace at 12.30am, and appears on the balcony for a flypast by the RAF at 1pm accompanied by another gun salute at the Tower of London. Tickets are allocated by ballot (for which there is a small charge) and are limited to two per application. Write, enclosing an SAE, before the end of February to: The Brigade Major (Trooping the Colour), Headquarters, Household Division, Chelsea Barracks, SW1H 8RF.

22 June

Changing the Guard

Buckingham Palace. 11.30am, daily until 31 July at least. On 5 & 12 June Guard Change will be at 4pm without music or ceremony. The Guard is also changed at Horse Guards, Mon-Sat 11am, Sun 10am. 5, 10, 12 & 14 June, Guard Change at 4pm.

Mid November

State Opening of Parliament

House of Lords. This ceremony is not open to the public. However, the Royal Processions and the Queen, possibly accompanied by the Duke of Edinburgh, in the Irish or Australian State Coach, can be viewed on the route along the Mall, through Horse Guards Parade & Arch, Whitehall and Parliament Square. They depart from Buckingham Palace at approximately 11am. The Imperial State Crown leaves the Palace in its own carriage at 10.37am. A Gun Salute is fired at Hyde Park at 11.15am (at 12am at the Tower of London) as the Queen arrives at the Sovereign's Entrance to the House of Lords. Ring the London Tourist Board's State Opening of Parliament's service on: (0839) 123413 nearer the time for dates (notification is usually received about four weeks in advance).

ACKNOWLEDGEMENTS

Front Cover Pictures: Tim Graham. Image Bank. Comstock. The Royal Commission © 1993 Her Majesty The Queen.
All photographs reproduced by kind permission of the Royal Collection © 1993 Her Majesty The Queen with exception of the following:
p4/5: Images Colour Library; p6/7/8/9: Mary Evans Picture Library, The Bridgeman Art Library; p10/11: R.H.P.L, Tim Graham, Mecky Fögeling; p12: Tim Graham; p13: Tim Graham, Camera Press; p14/15: Chorley & Handford; p16/17: Tim Graham; p70/71: © Photographers International Ltd., Camera Press; p76/79: Tim Graham; p81: Mary Evans Picture Library, The Bridgeman Art Library. p82: Tim Graham.
Illustration: Michael La Bouchard.